Hamish Sturgeon is a British writer, actor and teacher now based in Los Angeles. Acting credits range from major TV shows like *SWAT* for CBS, *Moving On & Hank Zipzer* for the BBC and feature films Flight World War II and American Boogeywoman. Theatre credits include *Twelfth Night, Closer* and *Time and the Conways*. Hamish recently completed the screenplay *The Night Anonymous. The Aquarium* is his first poetry collection.

Dedicated to my father, Brian Charles Sturgeon

Hamish Sturgeon

THE AQUARIUM

AUSTIN MACAULEY PUBLISHERS™
LONDON • CAMBRIDGE • NEW YORK • SHARJAH

Ordering Information
Quantity sales: Special discounts are available on quantity purchases by corporations, associations, and others. For details, contact the publisher at the address below.

Publisher's Cataloging-in-Publication data
Sturgeon, Hamish
The Aquarium

ISBN 9781647502492 (Paperback)
ISBN 9781647502485 (Hardback)
ISBN 9781647502508 (ePub e-book)

Library of Congress Control Number: 2021921723

www.austinmacauley.com/us

First Published 2022
Austin Macauley Publishers LLC
40 Wall Street, 33rd Floor, Suite 3302
New York, NY 10005
USA

mail-usa@austinmacauley.com
+1 (646) 5125767

Charles

The House

There is a long drive attached to this house
Sheltered by trees of the strongest oak
And bordered by fields of wild deer.
A certain window carved deep in the house is the best way
to see it.
On a clear day you can see the far distant road ahead,
Cars like little pellets.
People on the move. Work. Home.
I watch them from here. Sharp, knobbled elbow
Jabbing into an old cushion.
Worn. Faded. Dying.
Like the house.

The Music Room

I can see her now, Alice.
Fingers working the piano, her head rocking.
"Your head must be still," I said, "remember the rules?"
She looks up at me, startled.
Her eyes, the deepest blue, drown me.
She slows her playing and then stops.
Her profile caught in the afternoon sun,
Hair tousled, strands loose,
She lights a cigarette,
Looks out of the music room window,
And smiles.
Just to herself.

Birthday

The lights of the weaving, meandering cars hit the portico
roof,
An explosion of light flashing the front of the house
As they cluster in the circular drive.

The door cracks open,
The crunch of gravel on stubborn heels.
Giggling women, jeering men.
Soft thuds of car doors,
Engines sparking and purring.

I wait for Alice. I wait for her in the shadows, so much of
us in the dark.
Young lovers, supple bones.
Emerald green gown,
Gliding the floor.

Effortlessly.

Garden Party

It was every year in June,
Our garden party.
When the sun was always shining
And all the people came
From the village
To watch.

1949

Alice mothered our children like a blast wave,
Crashing through their innocence like atomic bullets,
Daily tasks of warfare rifling through their souls,
Barked orders at the Nanny,
Rounded bustling Tilly,
The diffident colonel sheltering her troops.

I watched, like I always watched,
The rubble of our family gently tapping at my boots
In the grounds of my adoration.
The war bombs
Were nothing
Compared
To the string attached to her sanity,
Her fading grace gently tugging at it.

Tightropes
Of
Tiny
Little
Valves.

Orangery

We were laughing
Together
At the newspapers
In the orangery,
The children playing on the lake,
Nervously watching us.
Their parents trapped in the sunlight,
Laughing together.

1990

15

Here they are, all grown
With their own children,
And still our history slowly bubbling
To nothing.

They will try to get me from this house
A certain duty to the bloodline
And I must resist them. Yes.
(A certain duty to the bloodline).

Estuary

She hurled the mirror at me with great force
Then started on the crockery.
Tears blazing soft trails, tiny rivers.
I dodged, and dodged, and dodged, laughing
I followed her through the corridors
Past the rooms laden with gilded furniture,
Her hair loose and flowing –
Until she stopped dead in the half-light
By the equestrian statue and
Looked at me,
Animal-like,
As she ripped off her dress
To fuck.

Dead Things

Dead things
Are bloodless and boneless,
But I saw her that day.
She swept into the library
In pure white silk
And caught the fading light with a single breath.

All I could do was follow her,
Swirled up in the vapors
Of her world,
Until she dropped
Into the depths –
Her translucency
A shimmering curtain
To the ever after.

Little Fishes

It was my ninth birthday.
I joined the other children playing,
Sharp shrieks and circling laughter
Catching me in the whoosh, whoosh, and whoosh.
Through the meadow grasses and down, down, down
To the sodden, squelching, burst banks of the river,
Where we, like little fishes, leaped and danced
The cold waters to submission.

Soaked through, we dripped our way back to the house,
My little heart heavy with delight
At the strange sensation of belonging.

Loss

The children left
In quick succession,
Not fastened to the house
In the slightest.
Alice spent months
Staring out of windows
Undressed and
Unhinged,
As though grasping for the word

Loss.

The Visit

The endless corridors extend themselves,
Intestinal.
I see you in the distance
Captured, birdlike,
Among strangers.
In your eyes, dogged defiance.
A familiar look.
Words that you dagger me with lodge themselves
Like tombstones. Edges sharp steel,
Pricked with your poison,
Nestling amongst my vital organs.
Visceral.
Indelible as this ink.
Irredeemable.
As irrefutable as your epitaph
(That I wrote you know…)

I still think of you moving into blackness,
Your years dripping into your pillow,
Tears like a light rain.

I wonder when you reach the forgotten house or
Wherever the dead crowd.

What of us will you share?

After You

This place is drenched in your absence.
On the blood pools of dried Claret,
On hand polished crystal,
In the flickering of the table lamp you chose,
In the hollow laughs of the guests
At your funeral –
Searching for narrative like hungry dogs –
I want to scream: "She is lost forever you fucking idiots,"
but
Instead
Grief lodged in me like brick,
I join the revelers,

Top their glasses –
A dutiful host.

Action

23

If I had wanted you dead,
I would have killed you myself;
Strong grip to the neck.
Wild eyes
Seeking life,
Fighting for it,
All in the name of action.
In all our years
Of silent suffering,
This act separated us.

Inheritance, 1931

24

That cold day lingered
Into the crisp night,
I watched from an upstairs window
The silent leaves fluttering
To the ground below.
If I were light, I thought,
If I were as light as a feather,
I should like very much
To blow away
And land
Somewhere
Completely
Different.
I thought of this till morning.

Maps

Those were the lost years
That drifted on a tail end of a dream.
Now, my crippled heart splutters
And spews out its guts,
Wrenching loose, grating against the sinew.
Those were the wasted times,
Seated on the edge of the living,
By the side of an idea,
Resting upon hope,
Along borders of my imagination.
A coast guard in a blustering sea.
Those days we let slip were the enemy.

Now shuffling through long empty rooms,
I trail the dust and map my routes
With gnarled hands.

I Remember the Day I Brought Alice Here

I am sitting in this squalid dark
Remembering the day
I brought Alice here.
I am throwing open the doors
To the long corridor.
Sunlight,
Floods the coffined halls,
Little beacons of light
Flashing her face.
She is young,
And the world was ours.
I follow her.
Happiness – fleeting –
And caught in the hooks
Of my expectation,
But still I hear her giggles
And still I see her hands trace the cracks
Of a broken gilded mirror,
Like she could piece it together with will itself.
Today, I will make my pilgrimage
To the edge of the lake
And remember the day I brought Alice here.

First Evening

8 pm

I long for the music to continue,
Sharp prods of rusty keys.
I squirm at the thundering crescendo
And swivel the ice in my drink –
Gathering ice caps – creaking.

9 pm

I glance across the room.
The ladies have gathered in their gowns
And are preparing for the next waltz.
Outside the rain falls,
Jabbing at the windows.
I move to stare at the wet dark.

10 pm

In the refection, I notice you.
Hands clapping in the air:
Delicate white glove slipping
Off your lap; clutching at sequins,
Pinned perilously to lemon chiffon.
And your laugh exploding the room.

12 pm

Rain pounds as you cower, shuddering
Under your raincoat, waiting to meet with me
Mouth to mouth,
And dig through wet clothes together
Whilst he parades the drawing room like a caged lion
Mourning missing prey.

After The Rain

I let you go, for now.
And you return to him.
Sweeping you move to leave,
Glittering in diamonds,
Buried under fur.

Suitor

Bloodied hand,
Knuckles bared, exposed white bone chipped.
White shirt. Stained heart red.
Tie twisted – a tiny knot.
He is floored, chugging giant blood gulps
Eyes bulging and arms flailing.
I watch for a while and hover over him
Until the blood surge calms.
I take small shallow breaths
And grab my dinner jacket,
Brush myself down,
Walk back into the house
To find Alice.
My underbelly
Soon to tame
The animal of my intentions.

Portrait

I was never enough for you. I think I always knew that. This crumbling decayed house knows it too. It started to pellet our love with decay from the off, and now it clings to me. A fly in a web, I can't shake. Our children are blind to so much. They do not see the trembling walls starting to stoop from the weight of its core and the gutters that spurt its remnants through the house. They see the wet damp, but not the tears. They see the long, windowless corridors but not that they are lined in the past, hundreds of spies. That they will share a space on that wall is lost to them, as it was to you. I cannot break links with the past. I tried. I tried for you. The large front hall – the heart of the house – the aorta. You are there, I put you there. Your portrait. It is luminous. You are resplendent, at peace with yourself – you are robust, solid, but you are also porcelain. Perhaps only I can see that though.

I like to think that you would only share that with me.

The Boat House

31

Alice was in there.
I had heard the wailing.
I pulled back the heavy wood doors.
Between two sailboats she had dropped herself into the deep
And called for death.
I pulled her back to me
Wet. Dripping. Heavy.

Dissolving

I was sitting in the study.
The room, blue with cold,
My hands clutching a stick
Festooned with the family crest.

Wind hurled itself through the house,
The front doors relinquishing their hold
And thrashing themselves open.
Swallows darting in-between the aged oak.

I dragged my way down the corridors
Long steady shuffles of tired feet,
Scraping the crimson walls.
The stick tap, tap, tapping.

Alice was standing there,
Dressed in silk and lace.
I stopped dead in my tracks.
"Come to me," she whispered, "come to me."

It was a trick. A trick of the mind.
That's what they all say, the aged mind,

But she was as clear as the daylight,
Until I went to reach her and she was already

Dissolving.

Safe

Alice was not faithful.
She was grasping at life, and I understood.
Our children were witnesses, bystanders,
And that I hated.
She, I think, did too.
I waited and waited for her to leave me,
To leave us.

She stayed
And persecuted herself further.
I thought for a while she loved me too much
And that I was the one she wanted to grow old with.
Or she was leaden with guilt for our babies.
Her instinct to nurture strained but intact.

I think she knew the truth was this:
I was the only one who would pull her from the boathouse.

Morning 1991

The air is thick with fog
On this wet winter morning,
And I have made tea to blister the cold.
I like the feel of the cold
Hands gripping the china, blood boiling.

The room is leaking.
Long straight lines of wet
Spurting through the cornice.
And I imagine it never stopping,
I imagine to drown in it.

My breath is short and
Chugs out spurts of smoky life
In little tiny pieces,
As I drag the coal box,
Heavier with each tug,
To capture the wet.

In the bowels of the house
The silence is pierced
By the thud of a piano.

One key that spoke of regret
Like no other could.

I am dreaming, I think
To myself, I am dreaming.
It is the sound of the past
Playing its victory game.
My God, it is a dagger.

1964

I found her.
As I always knew I would.

Her wild auburn hair
Floating matted.

Let me hold you
And your rigid body

           Will warm.

Had you wanted me to come earlier?
I will always wonder.

My Father Is Long Dead

My father is long dead,
But I see him stalking the rowan trees
In the orchard.
His own little army
Silenced,
Like his speech
From the bombs that exploded his world
And left him
Wrapped forever
In a steel shell. Mummified terror.
My father is long dead.

Open House

Here they come,
The day-trippers,
Crawling their way down the drive.
Picnic tables, folding chairs,
Cheese-filled sandwiches and
Darting children,
Sticks thrashing rhododendrons
Like lives depended on it.
This house was never yours,
They chant. A chorus of it.
"It is ours."
I think I agree.
Until I see Alice floating down the hall
Lost to the sound of the music
Playing in her mind.
Orchestras of light
That flows through her like electricity.
Then I say, as if a mantra from the window,
You may have the house,
The crumbling walls, shattered windows,
The long corridors of stale cold,
The portraits, the long dead, and dying.
You can claim it all with your

Little cards and a badge.
You can have the land, acres and acres of land.
The orchards –
Trees, my grandfather planted,
The meadowland and deer park.
You can have it all.
But not Alice.
Bobbing head floating in the boathouse.
I won't give you Alice.

Wedding Day

She was ivory, not white.
I was ivory, we were neither white.
Veiled she was given to me.
Underneath –
A shock of red rouge.

Here, but in Another Room

Here but in another room.
Though the silence is steely
And brave,
It is punctuated
By the hollow ticking of the grandfather clock.
Then, a cacophony of whispers,
The clutter of footsteps,
The clanging of conversation
And the surging of strangers
Swell the halls,
Treading the boards of the house.
They are claiming
Bit by rusty bit.
Stopped, for now, by the red cord,
A little sign saying "private."
Outside, dusk.
The bob of heads at the window.
And the cars, all those cars,
Little whirls.
Spitting gravel.

Winter Fall

43

The snow had fallen. I could sense it.
The joy of the whiteness, the extra lighted moon,
The children's shrieks, guttural.
Alice's laugh.
I rose to stare from the window
My family illuminated
By the blue white light.
Alice, momentous and electric,
Danced the snow,
Trailing our children. The huntress
Was solid that day,
Alive in the dark
Like an alley cat
Sequestering food.
I was alone, the voyeur,
The passing guest,
Glancing from the cold
Into a fire-lit room.
On the peripheral.
Incensed.

Leaving

The light is yellow
And frosted.
Shadows of shadows
Loom, then
Black dark
Pulling.
Pulling
Pulling.
A breath
Flickering
White,
Whiter,
Neon bright.
Orange
And blood-red lines,
Your faces –
Distorted, inhuman.
Blurry,
Grey,
Black.
Gone.

Berlin

I traipsed
Over
The dead
And
The
Dying
To get back to her.
Rose-pink with child,
She opened the house
To the war
Soldiered the wounded
And hand ploughed the land
Till it burnt.

Exiled

This is the end.
I am grieving
For the dusk light
In summer night's windows,
And the heated haze
Of night fires
Spreading the land like fog.
I imagine dead-heading
The last of the season's roses.
I am a strolling, shuffling
Man, content amongst the shadows.
Alone, but for the busy hum of
Night flies flickering electric in the darkening hue.
Then I see you lit by the log fire.
Your reflection in the neatly trimmed lawn
Enables me to shift on, regretfully,
Further and farther into the night.

Decay

Alice would never be old
Like me. Sagging face,
Heavy jowls, deep creviced wrinkles.
I knew you would burn out,
Just disappear, and I would be left to fester in this life
A good thirty years after you.
Body slowly decomposing,
Brittle bones, creaking
And urinary infections, leaking.
Stooped back, shorter.
The replay of memories.
Haunted. Visions of a long life.
You could never be old like me,
It would have killed you.

Night Bats

Naked we leapt into the fountain,
And I was giggling
And dripping
And the midges were gathering
To stick to our glue skins,
That you glazed with your kisses.
The night breeze brushed our skins
Like the touch of a ghost, feather-like,
And we stared into each other,
(The all-seeing stare of lovers)
Darting about the summer evening
Like night bats,
Fearless, but fragile in the
Blue-black dark.
We huddled together and counted
The stars, and the world was empty, for a short time,
Of all but us, and our cave
Nestling in the background.
We were all we would ever need.
Youth, actually, was all we would
Ever need.

The Dark

I am alone in the dark.
That was what you had said.
You were in the dark,
Wrestling in its infinite quiet,
Until suddenly
Out of nowhere
Like a sparkling diamond
You would reappear again.
A small smile and a twinkly eye.
Jazz seeping through
Cigarette smoke
Would be battery power to the children,
And we would dance
All giddy-hearted,
And I would fall in love with you again.
You were not alone in the dark,
We were all in the dark
Until you shone.

Spider's Path

Quiet company
Is the nest of spiders
That rest at my crippled feet
And shivered bones.

You are here,
A spirit body watching me
From the other chair.
A pity watch.
I reach for you.
Spiders scatter
Into the corners of the room.
Carried by rivers of lonely tears.

Care

51

I am left here
To the mercy
Of strangers
In their light blue
And crisp
Uniforms.
Clinical ubiquity but for
The tips of colored sneakers
That peer out.
Questioning?
Anonymous.
All of them.
Briskly moving
About the house,
Their pockets stretched
Filled with clumps
Of numbered
House keys –
Jangling
Shrill like.
The far distant cry
Of the

Forgotten
And the ever waiting.

Goldfish

53

From the moment we met, I had decided to love Alice.
She was wild-eyed and already partnered to the dramatic.
Incongruously beautiful. Long-limbed, ever graceful.
Her inherent nature more aligned with the animal world
than this.
Slightly adrift from convention, dislodged, but
Masked effortlessly in the finest silks,
The fit – always slightly off.
Almost enough to notice.
I took her home like a prize in a fayre,
A goldfish in a small polythene bag.
Its oxygen already depleted.

Alice

Fairytale, 1941

57

The house loomed ahead
As we lumbered toward it,
My cold hands
Trying to keep my wedding bouquet together.
He was watching me,
Searching for visible signs of joy,
I could feel it.
I was watching the creeping ivy
That clutched the house,
Its tendrils looping amongst the brick
To hoist itself, heaving, to reach the chimneys,
As if, perhaps, to strangle it.
I told myself again that I loved him,
And the baby inside me
That kicked a little,
Its tiny grasp
Clawing at me from inside,
Clutching itself to me like the ivy.

Flowers

58

Sentinels of sunflowers
At the foot of the drive.
I meander towards them,
Summer skirt flapping,
Charles
Watching me from the windows,
Blowing smoke.
Giving the picture
The haze it needed.

Bells

I am sitting, solitary,
In the window that faces
The front of the house,
The edge of the portico
Jabbing my eye
Like a lost particle.
I can hear the jangling of the bells
Tolling
Their way through the countryside,
Plucking at my nerves.
I am losing myself.
The waves start to convulse
And I am searching
For the faces of strangers.
Day staff at their business.
I turn the pages of a book.
The Bells…
Those Bells.

Doll

I knew when I married Charles
That I would let him down,
That my history would
Join us.
That I would start to unravel
Our love and play with it too hard, like a child
Dragging the head off a doll
With her teeth.
And I would hate him
As much as I would love him,
For all his kind words
And softness
I knew I would want him
To be rougher
Round the edges,
And I asked it of him,
I demanded it.
I wanted to be shaken
Like that doll. Its eyes rattled
And hair matted with blood.
Savaged.

The Night Watchman

I found myself draped
Cold pressed
Against granite countertops,
Amongst night scraps and meat trimmings
Watched by rickety racks of rancid
Pigs' heads –
Hung on tenterhooks,
A theatre show.

My cheek flesh
Scored –
Soldered across ice-caps
Of broken teeth –
And cracked bone.
Dried blood
Like a bruise
Deepening red
Swelling.

I had been taken by surprise.
He first had hit me –
A juggernaut –
As I had taken his

Dog for an evening walk.
He dragged me back,
Using clumps of hair,
Through to the
Parlour and empty kitchens.
The silence.
And then the scrape
Of the iron door
– Shutting.

My sixteen-year old bones
Had flailed and scratched
In the dark,
Hunting for the eyes
Of a black eyed
Monster.
To hook him – perhaps,
Like one of the pigs' heads.

Trails

63

Charles would always say
"I wish I could help you" and
"I don't know how to make it better."
I would think to myself,
I could just use some company,
Some inspired conversation
About the world and its inhabitants.
I could never communicate this,
Instead I would smile weakly and
Utter some conciliation,
Some piece of small talk
Easy to scatter, tiny breadcrumbs.
If he had really wanted, he could have followed them
And found the nugget of gold
At the end of a long, long trail.
I don't think he ever really wanted that journey.

Strange Birds

64

We are like two strange birds
Charles and I.
Strange birds
With decorated plumage.
A gilded cage,
The world watching.

Genes

My daughter looked like me
And I hated it.
It reminded me of all I was.
In a single smile
She could make me choke
And want to die.
I tried to hide it from her
But I think I failed.
She left me as soon as
She could
One day in December
Once the ice had thawed
Enough to release her into
The wild.
I spent every day thereafter,
Wishing she were here,
But that she looked more like her father.

Before Dawn

This crescent moon
Has fixed its smile,
With teeth clenched
And fists wrenched
Around my evening dress,
Stretched lifeless across the bedroom floor.
My shaking hands, varnished nails – chipped.
Reaches for the telephone,
The dial misty with cold,
I search for the numbers
To twist and turn, little poky holes – trapping fingers,
Until I give myself back to the light
And let the bed claim me.
Stretched limbless and empty.
Just like the dress.

Charles's Birthday Party, 1958

The guests were gathering
On the upper terrace.
Small huddles. Growing.
I watched from the bedroom window.

The house was bustling,
What staff remained
Settled into their pre-war roles
Tiny armies.

Through the house I charged,
Down the main hall and out
My dress trailing the floor
Little thorns, snagging.

Out to the terrace,
Layers and layers of them.
Small greetings,
Courtesies. Salutations.

Down the steps,
More groups merging towards me

Like swarms of little bees.
Seizing their chance.

Soldier

White skin. Delicate
Blue veins,
Scissor-like. Coursing.
Brave Soldier, brave man.
Give me your hand
And I will hold it.

Shared cigarettes
In the servant's quarters.
Empty rooms
Filled,
Long corridors linked
With rooms that pulsed
Into life.
Blood and fire.
Our secret love
Stored forever.

You had summoned me,
My soldier,
With your hollow leg.
You had summoned me
With a scratched note,

And there I was in the midst of the apple trees,
Beneath this burning sun.
Your touch had shaken me
And threatened my mettle.
Your scars were like winter trees
That mapped their way to me,
Etched in my memory,
I am forever changed.

Brave soldier. Brave man.
Give me your hand.

Last Evening

This is my last evening.
I can feel the sun from the bedroom window,
Large and warm but ever more slipping into the night,
Like a gentle arm tugging.
I am trying to move
This heavy head
Lodged between two pillows
Of the brightest white,
But it is leaden.
Charles is calling for me.
A distant echo, then louder, louder still.
His words, thunderous in my head, crowd closer, and closer
And my tears, bone shaking, convulsive sobs, uncontrolla-
ble surges,
Blister as they scrape the sides of my face.
Gentle knocks on the door, ever so gentle,
Tiny taps that render like a hammer to the head.
Vomit hurls through the palms of my hands,
Spraying the white sheets with crimson bile.
He is here. In the room. I can feel it.
I am groaning,
Crawling from the bed.
Screaming. Thrashing wildly.

Sinking into the sodden sheets.
He holds me.
I am fetal.

Quiet now, and ready.
This will be my last evening.

Laughter Lines

73

I used to trace the lines on your face
Growing like ice cracks.

You were so smart then,
You would leave me to the shadows.

You would let me track my way back
To our marriage.

We would entwine with each other
In the flickered flames of the drawing room.

And for a moment I would forgive my mother
For selling me wholesale to you.

I remember when you first came to track me down
In the first swell of our union.

And I would hate you,
For filling me with more guilt.

The wifeless man,
Who stretched the truth until it snapped.

Land Girls

The house had fed the town in the war
And we dug the land and made it breathe.
I had settled into the rhythm and
Yearned for it to continue.
I had loved the young wounded soldiers
More than my children
Because I could be useful to them.
I had fallen in love
And the house had creaked back into life.

The Hunter Storm

It was in the cut-grass smell
Of a late afternoon.
I was strolling in the garden,
Feet trailing damp, sodden leaves,
That I suddenly found myself
Breathing the air in great big chunks,
Volcanic nausea
Swelling sea-like. Choking.
Chest throbbing, bones racking,
I crawl my way back to the house
And to the soft coolness of my un-made bed
That will fold itself around me
And lead me to sleep.
The dinner gong echoes through the house,
Thunderous domes.
Children's shrieks whirring outside
As they play hide and seek.
I am now staring at myself in a cracked mirror,
Applying rouge in
Small circles,
Carving cheeks.
Charles's guests are gathering,
Dodging the children

With polite laughs of solid indifference,
Their sparkly gowns
Lighting the house
Like tiny ticking time bombs.
The throb of small talk –
Jack hammer to my head…
The muffled drone of the gramophone record
Charles has played
To coax me downstairs
Like a frightened dog.
Heavy gowned, I stand to leave the bedroom.
Gentle breeze from the open window.
Small gulps. Head splitting.
Hands shaking, gripping a tumbler.
Polished nails, luminous red.
Heels piercing the edges of my dress
Like tent pegs. Unsteady.
Glass smashes, a thousand shards.
I clutch at the splinters,
Veined hands,
Red-blood rivers
Wrapping themselves in the skirts of my gown.
I collapse.
Back to the door.

Dinner gong stops.

Charles retreats.

Cut Lip

77

Soldier's kiss
Was salt on my wounds
For a time. Nothing
Had felt more real.

Mother

78

I am my mother's only child.
I wear my dresses like her love.
Pretty and well made,
But disposable –
And weather-dependent.

Dancing Spoons

In the starch white of the stretched linen table cloth,
Shadows of the silver spoons dance with
Curled fingers gathering their spoils
From the selection of teatime party cakes.
My mother was pressing me, cold-eyed, deadly,
To feign interest in the babbling talk of dresses,
But I could do nothing
But stifle a laugh
At the pantomime table show.

Sunday, 1941

I remember the day it started.
It had found its way to me in the dark,
Hesitantly, button-lipped,
It hung itself upon my long-limbed
And fragile frame;
A rose-skinned raincoat.

It was a glorious summer day
A sun-day in 1941,
And we were down by the lake.
Translucent white toes dipping
Themselves gingerly in the
Olive brown of the cauldron waters.
Charles looked muscular
And taut,
White vest, dappled
In the shade of an aging oak.
I was in a sundress,
Rose flowers,
White laced collars.
I had reached back, allowed myself
To nestle among the pillowing weeds,
And shielded my head

From Charles's sprinkling of water beads.
Freckled face. Dripping.
Moments passed, perhaps seconds.
I watched an ant – raisin black and squalid –
Journey itself through spear-like blades of grass
On to my red-skinned arm.
With a colossal jolt,
I felt the gigantic, overwhelming
Meaninglessness of it all.
I remember the day it started.

It had hung itself resolutely upon my frame.

Soldier Leaving, 1945

82

Keep myself solid
My soldier had said
As he prepared to leave.
Small bag bulging.
Name tags – anonymous –like our love.
Charles summons me to the front door, insistent. Black-
eyed.
I walk. Small shakes. Leaning. My execution walk.

I take his hand, my soldier.
Firm grasp. Chest pounds.
His eyes – green and lovely – ready to leave I think.
"Thank you, Lady Marsh."
Can't respond. Gentle nod, eyes locked. Seconds.

Gravel crunches. Small turn. Little grimace.
Sad apologetic look.

Soldier.

I think you will be the end of me.

Mist

This land is splintered with ice
And the morning mist rises nitrogen-like.
Deathly vapors seep themselves into lungs
Built of steel and grains of dust.
From solid rocks we all become blood and rust.

The Fountain

There they were
Down by the fountain,
On the newly manicured lawns,
Taking their pictures
And looking up at the house.
Looking at me
Staring from the window,
Small chugs of smoke
From my cigarette
That they couldn't see.
Next to me is my soldier,
Strong and loyal,
Dressed in the finest
And playing jazz on the old gramophone.
Drinks waiting for fresh ice cubes,
Small kisses to the neck,
Little nibbles,
Lips touch, gentle
Smell of leather and musk.
I watch the people passing by
And then my soldier is gone,
Empty feeling,
Eyes filling, I watch him leave again,

Morphing into the crowds,

Eyes of strangers,

Fingers trailing in the fountain.

Jumping Off Place

I have waited an eternity
To shine a light
On this poky corner life.
Charles and I settled into infinite numb,
Contentment spreading
Like a cool blue sea
Over burning fires,
As I, with shaking legs, climb my way
To the top of the
Diving board.

Two World's Collide

Fidelio's Prisoners' Chorus
Is playing for me,
Lush symphonies exploding
As I head through the house
In an emerald green satin gown
That sweeps the floor.
I head for the curved central staircase
And see the portrait of Charles watching me as I
Gather myself. I smile at him
Before I turn to face the crowds
Waiting patiently in the entrance hall below.
Little heads, sheltering from the rain,
Examining the carved fireplace,
The licking flames
Logs slipping,
Small sparks.
A young woman, staring.
I almost think she can see me.
Our eyes lock,
She, I think, is startled.
I smile politely
And head through the portico.

The Letter

Soldier wrote to me
Once.
Flowery words,
Small apologies.
Unnecessary –
Lies really.
The truth of us –
A fleeting swallow
Trapped in the drawing room –
Had evaded him.
And he sipped tea
Under the delicate flapping wings.
And carefully opened
The french windows.

Soldier's Heart

Soldier said:
There will be days that you will think me dead.
And he would laugh as if to voice the words he never dared.
To be afraid is to chance the memories of the fallen.
If I am brave, but yet cast ashore amongst the turgid dreams
of other men,
I am nothing to the world but a soldier who fought and died.
So, for me to be saved, you must fly the flags for all of us.
Be the strong-held roots of a tree we are tearing down,
And I will hold myself up, tie myself to the mast of victory,
So that in the dark, sweat-filled nights of terror,
In the long after war years,
I'll think again on you.

The lady with the auburn hair and sad eyes,
Trapped in the battlefield of her life forever,
And I will once again understand the meaning of the word
Courageous.

Supernova

He was the first to open my eyes
To the glorious, messy, blood, and guts of it all.
The life and death of the pulsating liver red heart.
The ever-reaching attached mind
Losing itself in the carnage, a bloodthirsty animal
licking stained lips.
The stakes so unendingly high I could never fail to impale
Myself upon them.
Surrender will be at the last dawn. I will let it take me
To the opening of the widest blue-sky,
Shifting into day God-like and armed
To witness the truest nature of all this.
He will observe me, I think, from afar.
As if distanced from the fire he ignited,
But warming cold hands
On the supernova flames of our love.
He will perhaps never understand
That I am grateful. That I shall nestle
Amongst a galaxy of stars
Simply because he found me and exploded me to life.

Canvas

When I arrived at this house
Bundled with the linen box,
I had a canvas in front of me of
The most dazzling white and
Gradually with clumsy hands
And an impetuous heart,
I have splashed broad strokes
Of layered vermillion
In slippery black oil
All over it.
Little brittle
Charcoal stubs of life.
And now the truth remains –
Merely your version of our story.

In Memoriam

92

My grave is next to the boathouse.
A little white sign links me to the house

Forever.

Charles was kind,
He wrote simply this.

For my beloved Alice,
The place she was happiest.

www.ingramcontent.com/pod-product-compliance
Lightning Source LLC
Chambersburg PA
CBHW051815050726

47598CB00006B/2570